1,001

facts about

WILD ANIMALS

MOIRA BUTTERFIELD

Kingfisher Books

Contents

Produced by: Times Four Publishing Ltd
Edited by: Dee Turner
Additional text contributions: Catriona MacGregor
Designed by: Margaret Howdle, Chris Leishman and Brian Robertson
Cover design by: Terry Woodley
Illustrated by: Michael Steward, Sandra Hill, Ruth Lindsay, Shelagh McNicholas

Kingfisher Books, Grisewood & Dempsey Ltd,
Elsley House, 24-30 Great Titchfield Street,
London W1P 7AD

First published in paperback in 1993 by Kingfisher Books
10 9 8 7 6 5 4 3 2
Originally published in hardback in 1992 by Kingfisher Books

Copyright © Times Four Publishing Ltd 1992

BRITISH LIBRARY CATALOGUING IN PUBLICATION DATA
A catalogue record for this book is available from the British Library

ISBN 1 85697 030 2

Typeset by Amber Graphics, Burgess Hill.
Colour origination by RCS Graphics Ltd, Leeds.
Printed in Spain.

Introduction

This book is full of interesting facts about the animal kingdom. You can find out what the main animal groups are called and how they are different from each other. Or you can read about animals' homes and habitats, such as deserts, rainforests and oceans.

A special section will tell you about the world's endangered animals and the work that is being done to protect them. Find out, too, about some of the unusual and surprising ways that animals behave. There is even a section on some of the wild creatures that may be sharing your own home!

To help you pick out the things you want to read about, some key words are in bold type like this: **reptiles**.

Also, there are lots of easy-to-find facts beginning with a spot, like this:

● Snakes never close their eyes.

Across the top of each page there is a list of useful mini-facts – for example, the world's rarest animals, or the most dangerous sea creatures.

On each double page there is a Strange but True section containing especially unusual or startling facts.

On pages 42-45 you will find charts and lists of animal records and facts for you to refer to.

If you are not sure where to find facts about a particular topic, look in the Index on pages 46-48.

The Animal Kingdom

Animals are creatures that breathe in **oxygen**. They have to **eat** plants or other animals in order to survive.

Animals have been on the Earth in one form or another for about 700 million years. The first animals were tiny single-celled creatures.

Single-celled creatures

Today, several million different kinds of animals live on Earth. Scientists divide them into **related groups**.

Animal groups

Here are the main **animal groups**:

- Mammals (see p6) include such different examples as bats, whales, cats, kangaroos and humans. Many large creatures belong to this group.

- Reptiles (see p12) include snakes, lizards, turtles and crocodiles. Up to 65 million years ago, reptiles dominated the Earth as dinosaurs.

- Amphibians (see p12) have bodies that are adapted to live on land or in water. This group includes frogs, toads, newts and salamanders.

Strange but true

- The present day is sometimes called the 'Age of the Insects'. Insects vastly outnumber all the other animal groups.

- Because grass gives so little nourishment, cows must graze all day to get enough for their needs.

- Some scientists think that apes and humans are descended from a type of rodent, rather like a rat.

Animal food

Animals eat different kinds of **food**, depending on their size, the type of stomach they have and the food available.

- Animals that eat only plants are called herbivores.

- Animals that eat only meat are called carnivores.

Herbivorous zebra

Carnivorous lion

- Animals that eat both meat and plants are called omnivores.

- Predators help to strengthen the animal population. They tend to catch and kill the weakest members of an animal group. The strongest ones are left alive. These are more likely to breed healthy offspring.

Molluscs – slugs, snails, clams, octopuses

 Porifans – sea sponges

 Annelids – earthworms, ragworms

Echinoderms – starfish, sea-urchins

• Fish (see p10) are a large group of underwater creatures. This group includes such varied examples as sharks, seahorses and eels.

• The bird group (see p14) includes many different flying birds and some non-flying kinds. Examples of this group are found all over the world.

• Insects (see p 8) are by far the largest group of animals in the world today. They include ants, beetles, bees, butterflies, lice and flies.

• Arachnids have eight legs, in contrast to the six-legged insects. The arachnid group includes scorpions, harvestmen, mites and spiders.

The food chain

Animals are linked together by what they eat, forming a **food chain**. The smallest animals eat plants. They are in turn eaten by larger animals, and so on. Here is a typical food chain:

Plant (eaten by aphid)

Spider (eaten by small bird)

Bird of prey (the end of this chain)

Small bird (eaten by bird of prey)

Aphid (eaten by spider)

Mouse (eaten by bird of prey)

Mammals

Mammals are a very successful group of animals found all over the world. There are about **4050 species** in all.

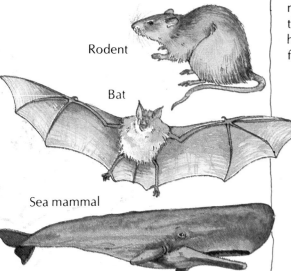

Rodent

Bat

Sea mammal

The mammal family includes **bats**, **rodents** (small gnawing creatures such as rats and mice) and some sea animals such as **whales** and **dolphins**. It also includes the **primates**. Human beings are part of the primate group, along with lemurs, monkeys and apes.

Primates

Mammal facts

Mammals have:

• Hairy bodies, to help them keep warm. Some mammals have thick fur; some only have a fine fur.

• Skulls and backbones. Animals with backbones are called vertebrates.

• Warm blood, which means that they can keep their own body temperature at a comfortable level.

• The ability to suckle their young, which means that they can feed babies with milk from their body.

Different kinds of mammal

Zoologists split mammals into three **scientific groups**. Each group gives birth to babies in a different way.

• Monotremes lay eggs and hatch their young. There are only two types of monotremes: the duck-billed platypus from Australia and the spiny anteaters or echidnas from Australia and New Guinea.

Duck-billed platypus

• Placental mammal babies are born alive and well-developed. When a placental baby is growing inside its mother it lives inside a kind of protective sac. Its blood supply is linked to its mother's.

• Marsupial mammal babies are born very tiny and undeveloped. Most marsupial babies finish growing inside pouches on their mother's body. Kangaroos are marsupials.

A human embryo

Baby in pouch

6

Giant panda (China)

Javan rhino (Java)

Mountain gorilla (Congo, Uganda)

Amazing mammals

Mammals are lots of different shapes and sizes. That is partly because they have developed to survive in many different kinds of places. Here are some **mammal record-breakers:**

• The world's noisiest land animals are South American howler monkeys. When the male monkeys call, their screams can be heard from 16 km away.

• The world's largest land mammal is the African elephant. Adult bull elephants grow over 3 metres tall and weigh about 5.7 tonnes.

• Cheetahs are the world's fastest animals on land. They can run up to 100 km/h over short distances.

• The giraffe is the tallest mammal in the world. It can grow over 5 metres. It has a long neck so that it can reach leaves high up in the trees.

Primates

Primates are the most well-developed mammals. They have:

• Complex brains, which means that they are able to think better than most other creatures in the animal kingdom.

• The ability to stand upright for long periods.

• More highly-developed hands than any other animal group. They can use their hands for all kinds of complicated skills.

• Eyes set side by side in the front of the head, which means that they can see more clearly than most other creatures.

Strange but true

• Many mammals sleep for long periods. Lions sleep up to 20 hours a day.

• Gorillas sleep in nests which they build in low branches of trees.

• Lions and tigers have been successfully crossed to make a new animal – the 'tigon'

• Blue whale babies weigh up to 7 tonnes at birth.

Insects

Insects are the biggest animal group. There are vast numbers of them, and there are probably many unknown types of insect still to be discovered.

Insects are found all over the world, even in frozen lands and in scorching deserts where other animals find it hard to survive.

Most insects live on their own for most of their lives, but some insects, such as bees, live in **organized communities** with many companions of the same type.

Insect parts

Insects do not all look the same, but they all have some characteristics in common. **All insects** have:

• A protective outer covering called an 'exoskeleton'. Insects are 'invertebrates', which means that they do not have backbones. They do have internal skeletons.

• A head which carries the eyes, antennae and feeding parts.

• An abdomen, made up of a series of segments. Vital organs such as the heart are inside.

• A thorax, which carries legs and sometimes wings.

Head

Thorax

Abdomen

Eye

• Three pairs of jointed legs.

• Cold blood, which means that they cannot control their own body temperature. They rely on the temperature of their surroundings to keep them alive.

• Many insects have compound eyes, made of hundreds of tiny lenses.

Strange but true

• Some butterflies have scented wings, to attract a mate.

• Some insects produce tiny lights on their bodies to attract mates.

• Crickets have ears positioned on their knees.

• Prehistoric dragonflies had wingspans up to 76 cm across, wider than many modern birds.

Growing up

Some insects go through a complete change of body and appearance called **metamorphosis**. There are four stages:

1. The female insect lays lots of tiny eggs, sometimes on the underside of a leaf.

2. The eggs hatch into larvae. Caterpillars, grubs and maggots are all forms of insect larvae.

3. When the larvae has grown enough it changes into a pupa (or chrysalis), inside a hard case called a cocoon, the insects' body dissolves and reforms into a new shape.

4. Once the change has occurred, the cocoon splits open and the adult insect comes out. Butterflies, moths, beetles, flies, ants and bees all go through metamorphosis.

Types of insect

The **insect world** is divided into groups. Here are some of them:

Honey bees

● Wasps and bees live in well-organized communities, where each insect has a particular job to do.

Cricket

● Crickets and grasshoppers have strong hind legs for jumping. They can rub parts of the body together to make a 'singing' sound that attracts a mate.

Dragonfly

● Dragonflies and damselflies have fierce jaws which they use to catch other flying insects such as flies.

● Bugs are insects with mouthparts made for sucking. Some bugs feed on plant juices; some feed on blood.

Blackfly bug

● Some bugs live in or on water. You can often see them walking over the surfaces of ponds.

Pond skater

● Flies have only one pair of wings, but they also have tiny balancing organs at the back of their bodies. These help them to land upside-down.

● Beetles are the biggest insect group. Their front wings are hard outer coverings for their back wings.

Stag beetle

● Butterflies and moths have tiny scales that cover their bodies. The scales are made up of thousands of tiny hairs.

Fish

Fish live in oceans, rivers, lakes and ponds. They are **cold-blooded**, which means that they cannot change their own body temperature.

There are about 20,000 different **species**, ranging from giant whale sharks about 12 metres long to dwarf gobies no bigger than a thumbnail.

Bony fish

Most fish belong to the **bony fish** group, which means that they have **bone skeletons** inside their bodies. Many of the fish we eat are of this kind.

- Bony fish have a gill slit on either side of the body. The slits are covered over with flaps of skin.

- Flat fish, such as plaice and sole, are bony. They lie on one side of their bodies.

Jawless fish

Lampreys and hagfish belong to the **jawless** fish group.

- Jawless fish have round sucking funnels for mouths. They have sharp teeth to hook onto their prey.

- Lampreys suck the blood of prey. Hagfish eat the flesh of their victims.

- Most bony fish have a little air-filled sac called a swim bladder inside their bodies. This bladder acts rather like water-wings; it keeps the fish floating in the water.

Fish facts

Most fish have:

- Backbones. All fish are vertebrates.

- A scaly skin, which stays moist and waterproof. Eels and lampreys are the only fish to have smooth skins.

- Gills, which are underneath slits or flaps of skin on either side of the head. When a fish opens its mouth water comes in and washes over the gills. They absorb oxygen from the water and pass it into the fish's body. Waste water goes out through the slits.

Strange but true

- Pufferfish can puff their bodies up to scare away enemies.

- Salmon live in the sea, but they return to breed in the river where they were born.

- There are probably about a trillion herring in the Atlantic Ocean (a million million million).

- A female cod can lay up to 9 million eggs.

Jawless fish mouth

Lamprey

Fishmeal (used in fertilizers)

Fish oil (used in various products)

Arrow heads and harpoon hooks (fish teeth)

Cartilaginous fish

The **cartilaginous** fish family includes sharks, rays, skate and dogfish. They have:

● Skeletons made of tough, gristly cartilage instead of bones.

● No swim bladders. This makes them heavier than water. They must keep swimming all the time, or they will sink.

● Fins and a tail that help the fish to steer through the water.

● A streamlined shape, which is smooth and curved. This makes it easier for the fish to slip smoothly through the water.

● Five gill slits on either side of the body. These are easy to see because they are not covered by skin flaps.

● A special sense called a 'lateral line', made of groups of cells which form a line along both sides of the body. The cells can feel changes of pressure in the water around them, caused by objects such as rocks and other fish.

Fish reproduction

Most female fish lay thousands of tiny **eggs** that float in the water. Many of the eggs are eaten by predators before they hatch.

● The male seahorse is unusual because it carries the eggs instead of the female. The female lays her eggs into a pouch on the male's body. When the babies hatch they stay in the pouch while they grow.

● Unlike most fish, tilapia look after their young. When its family is threatened this fish opens its mouth and its babies swim inside for safety.

● Skate and dogfish lay their eggs inside horny cases, which are known as mermaids' purses. Sometimes the old discarded cases can be found washed up on the beach.

11

Reptiles and Amphibians

Amphibians are a group of animals that spend part of their lives in water and part of their lives on land. **Frogs**, **toads**, **newts** and **salamanders** are all examples.

Amphibians

Reptiles live and breed mostly on land, although a few live in water. **Snakes**, **lizards**, **crocodiles** and **turtles** are all reptiles.

Reptiles

Amphibians

Amphibians have moist **slimy skin**. They always live near **fresh water** because they must return there in order to breed.

• There are swimming frogs, burrowing frogs, climbing frogs and even flying frogs that can glide from tree to tree.

• Like most amphibians, baby frogs metamorphose, which means that they change completely before they become adult (see p8). They grow from tiny tadpoles into frogs.

Spawn   Tadpole   Legs form   Frog

Reptiles

Reptiles are **cold-blooded**, which is why they need to live in warm climates. They have scaly, **waterproof skin** and most of them lay **eggs** with tough protective shells.

Lizards are reptiles with scaly bodies and four limbs:

• Some lizards have collars of skin which they puff out to make themselves look bigger when they are excited or scared.

Tortoises, **terrapins** and **turtles** are reptiles with protective shells.

Frilled lizard

• Turtles live in seawater. They only come ashore to lay their eggs.

• The largest, heaviest lizard is the komodo dragon from Indonesia. It can grow up to 3 metres long, and is a fierce hunter.

Komodo dragon

Hairy frog
(Central Africa)

Surinam toad
(S. America)

Horned Escuerzo
(S. America)

• Newts and salamanders are long, thin and lizard-like. There are many different types and colours.

Tiger salamander (N. America)

• There is a third small group of amphibians called caecilians. They are strange creatures that look more like earthworms. They spend their lives burrowing in sand and mud.

Mexican caecilian

Strange but true

• Snakes never close their eyes at any time.

• Chameleon lizards can look in two directions at once.

• If a lizard's tail is broken off, it can usually grow a new one.

• Ancient Egyptians thought crocodiles were sacred. They mummified (preserved) thousands of them.

Snakes are limbless reptiles.

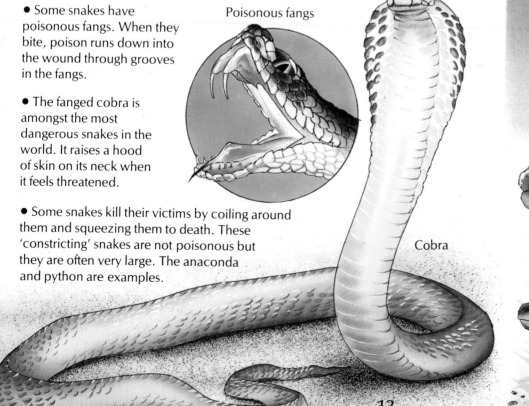

• Some snakes have poisonous fangs. When they bite, poison runs down into the wound through grooves in the fangs.

Poisonous fangs

• The fanged cobra is amongst the most dangerous snakes in the world. It raises a hood of skin on its neck when it feels threatened.

• Some snakes kill their victims by coiling around them and squeezing them to death. These 'constricting' snakes are not poisonous but they are often very large. The anaconda and python are examples.

Cobra

There are 120 species of **crocodiles** and **alligators**.

• The difference between the two is that when a crocodile's mouth is closed you can see its fourth tooth sticking out over the lower jaw.

Crocodiles

Birds

Birds are **warm-blooded** animals with **internal skeletons**. They all have **wings** and **feathers**, although not all birds can fly. There is a wide variety of birds. They live in many different habitats all over the world, from icy polar lands to hot tropical rainforests. Some birds live alone or in small groups. Others live in **colonies** numbering many thousands.

Bird facts

Most birds have bodies designed for flight. All **flying birds** have these physical features:

● A light, waterproof covering of feathers over most of the body. They help birds to fly and also keep body heat in, so the bird stays warm.

● A streamlined body shape. This helps birds to travel smoothly through the air by cutting down air resistance.

● Two wings covered with extra-strong flight feathers. The wings help to raise the bird into the air and the bird keeps itself aloft by flapping them.

● Scaly legs and feet with three or four toes and sharp claws.

● A horny pointed beak for feeding. Different birds have differently shaped beaks.

● Lightweight, partly hollow internal bones.

Strange but true

● The earliest known bird, called Archaeopteryx, lived 150 million years ago. Unlike modern birds it had teeth.

● Swifts spend almost all their lives in the air. They only land to breed.

● Flamingoes are pink because their bodies take on the pink colour of the shrimps they eat.

● The Andean sword-billed hummingbird has a beak longer than its body.

Eggs and nests

Bird species breed at certain times of the year, when the weather is mild and there is a good supply of food.

● Some male birds use complicated dances, special songs, or displays to attract females. For instance, the male peacock shows off its bright tail feathers to interest a mate.

Peacock male

● Eggs vary in colour and shape. For instance, some are speckled so that they are difficult to spot when they are lying in a nest.

Woodpecker – long beak for picking insects out of bark

Gannet – sharp bill for spearing fish

Parrot – powerful hooked beak for cracking seeds

Types of bird

Here are some different **bird groups:**

Osprey with fish

- Birds of prey (also called raptors) hunt other animals. They have curved talons for grasping prey, hooked beaks for tearing flesh and good eyesight to help them hunt. Eagles, owls and hawks are all birds of prey.

African ostrich

- Some bird species have lost the ability to fly. The world's largest bird, the African ostrich, is an example. It is too heavy to take off but it has powerful legs and can run as fast as 65 km/h.

Feathers

Bird feathers are made from **keratin**, a substance which is also found in hair and horn.

- Down the middle of a feather there is a stiff horny shaft called a quill.

- The flat part on either side of the quill is called the vane. It is made from tiny fibres called barbs. There are about 600 barbs on either side, each carrying smaller offshoots. All the barbs and offshoots are locked tightly together by hooks to make a smooth surface.

Quill

Vane

Barbs

- Water birds have long legs for wading. They often have webbed feet to help them paddle, and long bills or beaks for finding food in the water. Cormorants, ducks and flamingoes are examples of waterbirds.

Weaver bird's nest

A colony of flamingoes

- Most birds build nests where they lay eggs and hatch young. One of the most complicated examples is the carefully woven bell-shaped nest of the weaver bird, found in Africa and Australia.

15

Grassland Animals

Grasslands are wide, open areas where grasses and shrubs grow.

Temperate grasslands are found in cool parts of the world in the middle of large land masses, where rainfall is low. These areas are often used for cattle.

Tropical grassland is found mainly in Africa and South America. In Africa it is called **savanna**, and in South America it is called **pampas**. Here rain falls only in summer.

Tropical grassland provides a home for many wild animals.

Plant-eating animals

Most grassland animals are **grazers**, eating grass and other plants. Grazers live together in **herds**, for safety. They move about looking for fresh pastures and water pools. Here are some examples of plant-eaters on the **African savanna**:

● Antelope live in most tropical grassland areas. Species include oryx, eland and gazelles. Although they are only 60 cm tall, gazelles can run at 90 km/h to escape danger.

● The African savanna has shrubs and trees as well as grass. These provide food for giraffes, elephants and rhinos.

● Zebras move in large herds, often accompanied by wildebeest. While some zebras graze, others stay on the lookout for lions, their main enemy. Zebras can hear and smell better than most other grazing creatures.

Strange but true

● Elephants spend 23 hours a day eating.

● Some antelope can leap 3 metres in the air from a standing start.

● Vultures sometimes eat so much they can't take off again.

● No two zebras have exactly the same pattern of stripes. Like human fingerprints, each zebra pattern is unique.

Zebras prefer taller grasses

 Some antelope stand on their hind legs to reach low tree branches

 Giraffes and elephants eat the tops of trees

Meat-eaters

The main threat to the grassland plant-eaters are **meat-eaters** such as lions, leopards and hunting dogs.

- Lions live in groups called prides. They hunt and kill only when they are hungry. Antelope and zebras are their favourite food.

- African hunting dogs live in large, well-organized packs. They hunt together, separating weak or young animals from herds.

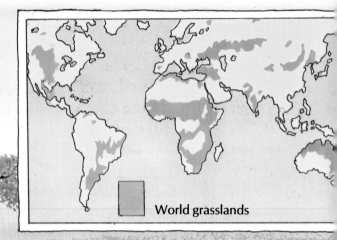

World grasslands

Scavengers

Scavengers are creatures who eat the leftovers from dead animal carcasses. When the grassland hunters have finished with their prey, the scavengers move in to pick the bones clean.

- Vultures are large birds found in many grassland areas of the world. They use their keen eyesight to spot dead animals far below them.

- Hyenas usually eat the remains of another animal's kill, but they will hunt if food is scarce. Their 'chuckling' hunting cry sounds rather like a human laugh.

- Although vultures and hyenas have a bad reputation, they provide a useful 'garbage disposal' service, because if carcasses are left to rot they attract flies and disease.

Rainforest Animals

Javan rhino

Rainforests are hot, steamy jungles that grow in areas on either side of the Equator – an imaginary line that circles the middle of the Earth. Rainforest areas have **high temperatures** and **heavy rainfall** all the year round. They are the richest animal and plant habitats in the world.

Equator

Rainforest area

Strange but true

- The African jungle okapi's tongue is so long, it can be used to lick the creature's eyes.

- The African giant snail grows up to 39 cm long.

- The strongest-known animal poison comes from the arrow-poison frog.

- The Amazon 'Jesus Christ lizard' can run across water.

Rainforest birds

Many **birds** make their home in the rainforest trees.

- Each forest region has its own giant eagle species. These birds build huge twig platforms on top of the highest trees.

Horn

Toucan

- Brightly-coloured macaws, hornbills and toucans make their nests in holes in tree trunks.

Mac

- There are lots of different hummingbird species in the Amazon region. They hover by flowers, drinking the sweet nectar with their long beaks. They beat their wings between 50 and 80 times a second.

Hummingbird

Rainforest insects

There are many, many thousands of different insect species in the rainforests.

- Ants can be found everywhere in the rainforests. Huge columns of fierce army ants travel through the forest areas of Central America, destroying everything in their path.

- Giant butterflies flit amongst the trees. Many of them are brightly-coloured. This is a signal that they taste horrible.

18

Gliders

- The Asian flying squirrel glides from tree to tree using the skin stretched between its legs like a parachute.

Flying squirrel

Flying snake

- When the flying snake launches itself, it flattens its body into a broad ribbon shape so that it can glide through the air.

Animals in the trees

Most rainforest **mammals** live up in the tree branches.

- The Amazon sloth hangs motionless and upside down for days on end. It has a shaggy coat and long claws for gripping branches.

Sloth

Margay

Ocelot

- There are lots of different jungle monkeys. Some of them have prehensile tails, which can be used like a hand to grip on to things.

- The Amazon margay and the ocelot are types of rainforest cat. Both are expert tree climbers.

Reptiles

Rainforests make ideal homes for warmth-loving **reptiles**.

- The world's biggest insect, the Goliath beetle, lives in African rainforests.

- The bushmaster snake lives amongst tree branches. It has heat-sensitive patches on its head, so it can find possible victims by sensing their body heat. Its bite can kill humans.

- The world's heaviest snake is the anaconda, found in South America and Trinidad. It can weigh up to 150 kg, and strangles its prey by coiling around it. It feeds mainly on birds, deer and rodents.

Desert Animals

About one eighth of the Earth's surface is **desert**. A desert is an area where less than 25 cm of rain falls on average each year.

Some deserts are very cold in winter. Others are hot all the year round, with high temperatures during the day and cooler temperatures at night.

Most desert animals tend to come out at night, staying out of the daytime heat by sheltering under rocks or in their underground burrows.

The major problem of desert survival is **lack of water**. Many animals are cleverly adapted to cope with the drought.

Snakes and lizards

Snakes and **lizards** are cold-blooded (see p12) and need the Sun's heat in order to survive. Deserts are ideal homes for them.

● There are many different kinds of American rattlesnake, most of them highly poisonous. When a rattlesnake is angry, it makes a warning rattle by shaking scales positioned on the end of its tail.

● Sidewinder snakes have developed an efficient way of travelling over soft sand. They use their bodies to lever themselves along, leaving trails of wavy lines behind them on the sand.

Rattlesnake

Sidewinder snake

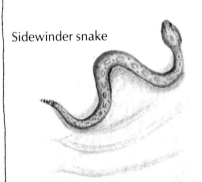

Amphibians

● The American spadefoot toad burrows underground during hot weather. It can stay buried for up to 11 months because its waterproof coat keeps moisture in its body. When rain arrives, the toads come out to breed.

Insects and spiders

There are many different **desert insects** and **spiders**.

● When it rains, the eggs of bugs, beeties and butterflies hatch, after lying dormant for many months.

● Most desert spiders are hunters. They do not use webs to trap prey. Instead they search for creatures to attack.

● A Namib Desert darkling beetle collects water from sea fog that rolls in from the nearby Atlantic. The fog condenses on the beetle's body and runs into its mouth.

Darkling beetle

Red-kneed tarantula (Mexico)

Bighorn sheep (USA): can store water in its stomach

Desert tortoise (USA): keeps cool by licking its head and neck

Moloch lizard (Australia): can condense water from the air onto its skin

Desert mammals

Desert mammals usually stay out of the daytime heat, in order to conserve water. Many of the smaller mammals never drink, getting all the moisture they need from seeds, shoots, or other creatures.

● The Saharan fennec fox has especially big ears that help to keep it cool. Blood vessels run near the skin surface of the ears, giving off heat as air blows across them.

Saharan fennec fox

Kangaroo rat

● The most common desert mammals are rodents. The kangaroo rat is an example. It stores plant seeds deep in its burrow, leaving them to collect moisture from the soil. This way, the rat gets a ready supply of water.

● Camels can survive for many days without regular water or food. They have wide, hairy feet to stop them sinking in the sand, and their nostrils can close up to keep out dust.

One-humped dromedary

Desert birds

Gila woodpecker

Most **desert birds** shelter from the daytime heat beneath rocks or plants.

● The saguaro cactus is found in the Sonoran desert in south-west USA. It can grow up to 15 metres high, and provides a home for several desert birds. Gila woodpeckers peck out nest holes in the rubbery cactus flesh. Tiny elf owls nest in vacant holes and cactus wrens nest in forks.

Cactus wren

● The emu is found in Australian desert regions. It is the world's second largest bird (after the ostrich). It grows up to 1.7 metres high, and although it cannot fly it can run up to 64 km/h over short distances.

Elf owl

● Roadrunners are found in Mexico and Arizona. They are famous for their speed. They can run up to 37 km/h to catch snakes and lizards.

Roadrunner

Northern Forest Animals

Here are some small creatures to be found on the forest floor:

Ant

In northern parts of the world there are areas of cool forest which provide a home for all sorts of different creatures.

There are two types of cool forest. In warmer areas the trees are mainly deciduous, which means they shed their leaves in winter. In cold areas the trees are mainly coniferous, which means they have long-lasting needles instead of leaves.

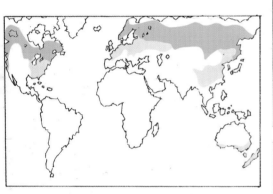

Coniferous forest
Deciduous forest

Many forest creatures are very shy and will hide if they hear strange noises. A good time to spot forest wildlife is at dusk or very early in the morning, when the animals tend to feed.

Deciduous woods

Deciduous trees have widely-spread branches. The gaps between their leaves allow plenty of sunlight through to the forest floor, where lots of plants grow and provide food for animals.

● Foxes live in burrows called 'earths'. They survive well in the forest because they will eat most things and they have very few enemies. During the daytime they lie low. During the night they hunt for birds, rodents and rabbits.

● The wood mouse is one of the most common forest rodents. It has long front teeth for gnawing through wood and nutshells.

Coniferous forests

Trees in coniferous forests are densely packed together. Very little light penetrates to the poor soil beneath, so there are few small plants. There is less animal life than in deciduous forests because there is less to eat.

● Martens have long bodies and short legs. There are several different species, including the pine marten.

Pine marten

● Red deer are common in northern forests. Male deer (stags) have long antlers covered in soft velvet. Each year the antlers drop off and a new pair grows.

Woodlouse

Centipede

Pill millipede

Snail

Bark beetle

● Lots of different insect-eating birds find food amongst the trees.

● Badgers are timid night time creatures. They can see well in the dark and have a strong sense of smell, so it is difficult to watch them without disturbing them.

● Caterpillars and insects feed off the tree leaves, while bark beetles bore into the trunks.

● Wild rabbits live in large groups in complicated tunnel networks called 'warrens'.

● Woodpeckers have strong beaks for drilling nest holes in tree trunks. They can sometimes be heard hammering on wood.

● A squirrel can leap 4 or 5 metres from branch to branch quite effortlessly, using its powerful hind legs to launch itself into the air. It uses its outstretched tail like a rudder, to steer its flight.

Strange but true

● The woodpecker has an extra-strong shock-resistant skull.

● Wood ants squirt powerful formic acid at their enemies.

● Male stags must not be approached when they call during the mating season, as they are liable to attack anyone nearby, mistaking them for a rival.

● Squirrels sometimes wrap their bushy tails around themselves to keep warm.

Mountain Animals

Here are some mountain animals from around the world:

Chinchilla (S. America)

Some animals are adapted to survive the harsh weather conditions often found in **mountains**.

The higher you go, the colder and wetter the climate becomes. Mountain animals tend to have **thick furry coats** or **extra layers of fat** to keep them warm.

Rocky Mountain goat
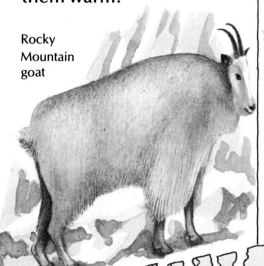

Strange but true

● The cougar can jump as high as 5 metres from a standing position.

● High in the mountains the level of oxygen in the air gets less, so some animals have larger hearts and lungs than normal, to compensate.

● A griffon vulture once crashed into an aircraft at the amazing height of 10,800 metres above ground level.

Mountain animals

● Yaks have long, thick coats to keep them warm in the Himalayan Mountains in Tibet. Sometimes they graze at heights above 4500 metres, making them the highest-living land animals.

Yak

● Llamas and vicuna belong to the camel family. They are farmed for wool and meat by the Quechua Indians high up in the Andean mountains of South America.

Llama

● The spectacled bear lives in the Andes Mountains. It gets its name from round facial markings.

Spectacled bear

● The Apollo butterfly lives high up in mountainous regions across the world. Spiders are found high up, too. However, it is usually too cold for reptiles and amphibians to survive.

Apollo butterfly

● Cougars (also called pumas or panthers) live in the mountain forests of America. They are very strong, powerful animals and can travel hundreds of kilometres a week in search of food.

Cougar
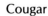

● Rocky Mountain goats are experts at climbing steep rocks. They have hoof pads which give them extra grip and allow them to climb up almost vertical surfaces. Their toes are shaped like pincers to help them get a firm footing.

● The chamois goat can climb very quickly. It has been known to climb over 1000 metres in 15 minutes.

Chamois

24

• The bobcat hunts small animals in the mountainous regions of North America and Mexico. During the breeding season it makes eerie screaming sounds.

Bobcat

High flyers

Many mountain birds are **raptors**, or birds of prey (see p15).

• The Andean condor is the world's largest bird of prey, weighing as much as 12 kg. It has a wingspan of about 3 metres. Like its relatives the vultures, it is a scavenger, which means it feeds on animal carcasses (see p17).

Andean condor

Golden eagle

Coping in the cold

In the winter months, when the weather is at its fiercest and food is hard to find, some mountain animals **hibernate**, which means that they sleep deeply for a long time. During hibernation:

• Body temperature drops.

Hibernating mountain hare

• The animal's heartbeat slows down, so that it uses up less energy.

• The body's fat reserves are gradually used up for nutrition.

• Eagles can fly very high. They glide on warm air currents called thermals to help lift them higher. Remains of Steppe eagles have been found on Mount Everest at heights of 7500 metres. It is thought that some eagles even fly right over Mount Everest.

25

Polar Animals

Here are some adaptations that polar animals have for living in the cold:

Arctic wolverine – two layers of fur

At the far south of the Earth there is a large area of land called **Antarctica**. It is always frozen over with ice.

Most Antarctic animals are **seabirds** and **ocean creatures** such as seals and fish.

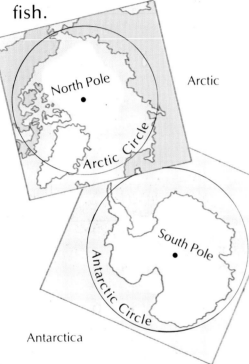

North Pole

Arctic

Arctic Circle

South Pole

Antarctic Circle

Antarctica

The **Arctic** is the area at the far north of the Earth. The Arctic Ocean is in the middle, covered by a huge floating sheet of ice.

Within the Arctic Circle there is barren land called **tundra**, where most of the Arctic animals live.

Arctic tundra animals

Most animals only come to the Arctic tundra during the short **summer months** and **migrate south** when winter comes. A few species brave the winter blizzards. Some of them burrow underground to wait for warmer temperatures in spring.

● Musk oxen are gentle creatures with warm, shaggy coats. They live in family groups which wander the tundra grazing on grasses. They stay on the tundra in winter.

Musk oxen

● Lemmings are the commonest small tundra animals. They are part of the rodent family. They live in underground burrows during winter and come up to the surface to feed in summer.

Lemming

● Polar bears are the fiercest Arctic animals. They stay all year round, hunting for seals. They can swim and dive well and they can sniff the scent of prey from several kilometres away. Male polar bears spend most of the time on their own. Female bears look after their cubs for a year or so.

● In summer, big herds of caribou (also called reindeer) travel up to the tundra from North America and Scandinavia.

Caribou

Polar bears

Arctic whales

● Bowheads are baleen whales. Instead of teeth they have curtains of bony strips. As a whale swims along, the strips sieve the water, collecting tiny shrimp-like krill to eat.

● The beluga is a toothed whale, so it doesn't rely on krill for its food. It feeds on fish at the floe-edge, which is the place where the Arctic pack-ice meets the sea.

Narwhal

● Male narwhals grow long spiralling tusks. They are sometimes nicknamed sea-unicorns.

Beluga

Bowhead

Arctic hare – fur turns white in winter

Seals – lots of fat to keep the cold out

Arctic fox – small body to limit heat loss

Arctic birds

Lots of **seabirds** migrate to the Arctic in summer.

● More than half a million seabird pairs nest in summer on the cliffs of Prince Leopold Island, in the Canadian Arctic.

Seabird

Antarctic animals

Since most of the Antarctic is covered in ice, there are very few land animals. But the oceans are rich in **fish**, **squid** and **krill**, providing plenty of food for other sea creatures. In the Antarctic Ocean region there are:

● Fish that produce a natural kind of anti-freeze to protect themselves from the extremely cold temperatures underwater.

Antarctic fish

● Blue whales, the world's biggest, heaviest living creatures. They can grow up to 30 metres long. They feed through baleen plates.

● Seven different types of Antarctic seal. They swim under the ice and saw through it with their teeth to make breathing holes that go up to the surface.

Crabeater seal

● Very few inland animals. The only ones are flies, mites, lice, fleas and tiny microbes. Mites are the most southerly-living animals on Earth.

Blue whale

Albatross

● Giant albatross seabirds, which come to the Antarctic coast to breed. They can live for up to 70 or 80 years.

● Several different types of penguin. The biggest one is the emperor penguin, which breeds in large colonies.

Emperor penguin with chick

Strange but true

● The biggest Antarctic inland animal is a wingless fly measuring about 60 mm long.

● Antarctic squid can grow up to 20 metres long. Many of them are cannibals – they attack and eat other squid.

Arctic seals

Seals sit on the Arctic ice-floes or swim in the ocean looking for fish to eat.

Ringed seal

Bearded seal

Undersea Animals

The **oceans** provide one of the largest wildlife habitats in the world. They cover about 70 per cent of the Earth's surface, and animals live in almost every part.

Ocean communities vary depending on the temperature and depth of the sea. Animals that live near the water surface are quite different from those that live deeper down.

Coral reefs and seaweed forests provide specialized habitats for particular kinds of creatures.

Ocean food

Ocean creatures have their own **food chain** (see p5):

● The food chain begins with tiny floating plants called phytoplankton. They float around in the seawater, near the surface. They are eaten by microscopic floating creatures called zooplankton.

Magnified zooplankton

● The zooplankton are eaten by small fish, which often travel around in groups called shoals.

● Baleen whales bypass part of the food chain and eat zooplankton (see p26).

● The small fish are eaten in their turn by larger fish, such as tuna.

● Some of the larger fish are eaten by humans.

Coral reefs

Coral reefs are made up of many thousands of individual animals called **polyps**. There are two kinds of corals: **hard** and **soft**.

● A coral polyp is a cylinder-shaped animal with a ring of tentacles. It takes calcium carbonate from the water and makes it into limestone.

A coral polyp

● Hard corals build up a hard wall of limestone around themselves. As the polyps grow and increase, a reef grows.

● Soft corals have a soft layer of tissue on the outside of a central rod.

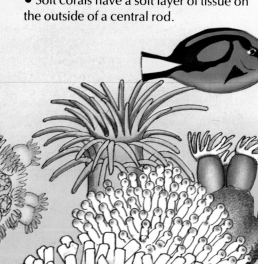

Stingray: poisonous tail spine

Stonefish: poisonous spines

Blue-ringed octopus: deadly bite

Unusual fish

Here are some examples of **unusual ocean fish**:

• The sawfish is found in warm oceans. It has a long flattened snout with toothed edges. As the fish moves along, it swings its saw from side to side, stunning and wounding small fish which it then eats. It is harmless to humans.

Sawfish

Bridal burrfish

• The wobbegong is an unusual shark found off Australia, China and Japan. Its skin is nobbly and fringed like seaweed, so that it can lie unseen on the seabed.

Wobbegong

• The Atlantic trumpetfish is a clever hunter. Its body is long and thin, and it hovers upside down in long seaweed, swaying so that tasty shrimps and small fish mistake it for a plant.

Trumpetfish

• The bridal burrfish lives on coral reefs. It has a round body covered in sharp spikes. When it needs to defend itself, it inflates into a spiky ball that makes it look twice its original size.

The ocean depths

Many areas of the ocean are too **deep** for sunlight to reach. Some creatures have adapted to life in the darkness.

• Some deepsea fish carry their own lights around, to confuse their enemies or to attract prey. For instance, the viperfish has a luminous pattern along its body.

Viperfish

• The female deepsea anglerfish has tentacles on her body. At the tip of each tentacle there is a shining lure designed to look like food for smaller fish. The anglerfish lies on the seabed, waiting to gulp down any unsuspecting prey.

Anglerfish

Strange but true

• Corals attack each other with stinging cells, in order to gain more territory.

• Sailors have been known to mistake basking whales for islands and try to land on them.

• Some tiny male anglerfish live permanently attached to the larger female.

• Giant-sized worms, crabs and clams live near underwater volcanic areas.

29

Wildlife in the Home

You may not realize it, but you could be sharing your house with wild animals. Houses are good **hunting grounds** and **nesting places** for a variety of creatures, and they provide food stores, too.

Although modern houses tend to be too clean and dry for some pests, it is not unusual to find the occasional beetle, moth, woodlouse, fly or spider in your home.

Parasites

Parasites are creatures that depend completely on other animals to survive. They often feed on blood.

● Bed bugs grow to about 4 mm long. By day they hide in warm dark places such as mattresses. At night, they come out to feed on their victim, leaving tiny itchy bites.

● Fleas leave itchy swelling bites. Human fleas are not very common, but cat and dog fleas will occasionally bite people.

Bed bug, magnified many times

Flea, magnified many times

● If you vacuum your bed mattress regularly, you won't be visited by bed bugs. However, if you have cats or dogs, you will sometimes get a flea.

Furniture and fabric eaters

Some small house creatures like to eat **wood** and **fabric**. They find a perfect supply of food in furniture, carpets, curtains and clothes.

● Furniture beetles lay their eggs in the crevices of damp wood. When the eggs hatch, the larvae (called woodworm) eat their way to the surface, making tiny tunnels.

● Clothes moths eat feathers, fur and wool. They live in damp, dark places such as cupboards and old chests and they lay their eggs on clothes or old carpeting.

● Bookworms are beetle larvae that live on paper. They like damp paper best.

● Woodlice like to eat damp paper. They breathe through gills on their legs. The gills must be kept wet, so woodlice live in damp places.

● Carpet beetles lay their eggs amongst carpet fluff. When the larvae hatch they are called 'woolly bears'. They eat feathers, dead insects, fur and wool.

Hunters

Some house creatures spend their time looking for smaller animals to capture and eat. These **hunters** help to keep the insect population down.

● A house spider's home is usually a sheet of webbing built in a shadowy corner. The spider lives in a silk tube built at the edge of the web. The threads in the web are sticky and trap flying insects, which make the web shake, and the spider then rushes out to kill them.

False scorpion, magnified

● False scorpions often live in house cellars, amongst piles of damp paper. Although they are small, they are fierce insect hunters.

Strange but true

● Fleas can jump up to 30 cm, twenty times their own body length.

● Bluebottle flies can smell meat from distances 7 km away.

● There are flour mites, prune mites, biscuit mites, chocolate mites and even cheese mites.

● House mice prefer chocolate, nuts, seeds and cereals to cheese.

Food stealers

Some creatures are out to steal **your food**. An estimated 15 per cent of all stored food ends up inside insects or rodents.

● Food mites are about the size of dust specks. They like to live on stale, damp food that is left at room temperature – inside a larder, for example.

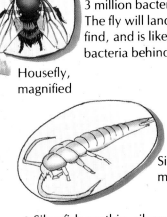

● There are an estimated 3 million bacteria on one housefly. The fly will land on any food it can find, and is likely to leave some bacteria behind when it leaves.

Housefly, magnified

● House mice live in dark, secret places such as lofts and cellars. They like to eat bread and cereals, but they will occasionally eat more unusual items such as soap and candles!

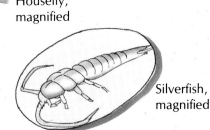

Bed mite, magnified

Silverfish, magnified

● The tiny bed mite eats the scales that constantly fall from human skin. It is widespread but harmless.

● Silverfish are thin, silvery insects about 1 cm long. They live in crevices in bathrooms and kitchens, and come out at night to look for food scraps.

31

Animal Babies

Pregnancies vary in length. Here are some mammal examples:

Golden hamster: two and a half weeks

All animal species produce **new generations**. Most species reproduce when the climate and food supply is right. For instance, many birds hatch new families in spring, when there is plenty of food to eat.

Within the animal kingdom there are many different kinds of **babies** and methods of **giving birth**.

Strange but true

● Grey tree frogs build nests of foam hanging over water. The tadpoles drop out of the foam when they hatch.

● The ichneumon fly injects its eggs into a caterpillar. The larvae hatch and eat their way out.

● Bacteria divide themselves once every 30 minutes or so.

Babies and parents

Some animals are good **parents**, protecting their babies and teaching them survival skills. However, the majority of creatures give no parental care at all.

● Most fish, amphibians and reptiles lay their eggs and then abandon them. Female fish lay their eggs in the water. Many cannot recognize their own eggs and they often eat them later.

Baby alligator

● The South American discus fish is a good parent. It makes sure that its newborn babies stay close to it for protection, by producing a tasty skin secretion which the babies eat.

● Crocodiles and alligators are caring parents. The female digs a pit, lays her eggs and then covers them with vegetation. When the babies hatch they squeal at the mother to dig them out.

Discus fish

● Mammal mothers feed and tend their young. For instance, most monkeys carry their babies with them wherever they go. The babies hold on to the mothers' fur.

● The female midwife toad lays a string of eggs on land. The male then carries the string wrapped around his back legs. When they are ready to hatch he takes the eggs to the water.

Male midwife toad

● Young domestic fowl chicks must teach themselves to feed. They begin by pecking at everything on the ground, including their own toes! Gradually they learn which things are the best to eat.

● Some cuckoos do not look after their own chicks. Instead they lay a single egg in a smaller bird's nest. The cuckoo hatches and pushes the other chicks out. Then it takes all the food the unwitting parent brings.

Cuckoo chick

Ways of reproducing

Here are the four basic ways that animals **reproduce**:

● The simplest forms of one-celled animals, such as amoebae, reproduce by splitting themselves in half to form two identical creatures. Animals that behave in this way are called asexual.

An amoeba splits in two

A hydra buds to make a new hydra

● Most animals have different male and female species. The male produces cells called sperm. The female produces egg cells called ova. The male sperm must join with the female egg before a new animal is produced. This method is called sexual reproduction.

Hermaphrodite worm

● Some simple animals, such as sea corals and freshwater hydra, produce new creatures by 'budding'. They grow a new branch which is a small version of the parent. Eventually the branch splits off to become a new individual.

Female egg   Male sperm

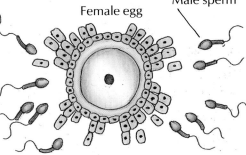

● Earthworms and some snails are hermaphrodite. This means that each animal is both male and female, and can produce both sperm and eggs. However, hermaphrodites still have to pair with each other in order to reproduce new creatures.

Eggs and babies

An egg is **fertilized** by a sperm in sexual reproduction. Once this occurs, the egg starts to develop into a new animal.

● Some animals, including most mammals, develop inside their mother's body before they are born. For instance, a newborn foal looks like a miniature version of its parent, and can walk almost immediately.

● Creatures such as birds and many insects lay their eggs once they are fertilized. The babies then develop inside the egg.

33

Camouflage

Camouflage is a pattern or colouring that **disguises** an animal so that it can hide from enemies, or creep up unseen on prey.

Camouflaged animals blend in with their surroundings. For instance, young deer usually have white spot markings that make them harder to see in the dappled light of a forest.

Some animals, such as the zebra, have vivid skin patterns that blur their outlines and make them hard for predators to see.

Changing colour

Some animals can **change colour** to match different backgrounds. Here are some examples:

• The Arctic fox, snowshoe rabbit and ptarmigan live on the Arctic tundra all year round (see p26). In winter they turn white to blend in with the snow and in summer they change back to darker colours.

Ptarmigan's winter coat

Ptarmigan's summer coat

• The cuttlefish changes colour as it swims over different plants and rocks. It has sacs of colour pigment in its skin. They expand or contract to produce a wide variety of shades.

Cuttlefish

Master of disguise

The **chameleon** is one of the animal kingdom's masters of disguise. It can change colour very quickly.

• The chameleon has colour cells called chromatophores in its body. Brain signals make the cells smaller or larger to alter the reptile's skin colour.

Chromatophores

Nerves in the spine relay brain signals.

Tricking enemies

These animals fool their enemies by looking like **fiercer creatures**:

- Many butterflies have false eyes on their wings to make them look like a much larger animal.

- The hawkmoth caterpillar is disguised to look like a deadly viper. When it is threatened it puffs itself up to show a false snake's head.

- The king snake is coloured with red, yellow and black rings to make it look like the much deadlier coral snake.

Strange but true

- Sloths let green algae grow on their hair as camouflage.

- A chameleon's colour can alter depending on its mood. In general, the calmer it is the paler it is.

- A nightjar on its ground nest looks just like a branch. Unfortunately, its camouflage is so good that it sometimes gets stepped on.

Sea colour

Creatures that live in the open sea or in cool waters tend to be dull in colour, whilst those that live in warmer waters are often brightly coloured. Many have startling patterns, too.

- The sea dragon is camouflaged to mimic seaweed. It has skin extensions which look like the long strands of weed it swims through.

Sea dragon

Stonefish

- The poisonous stonefish lives in warm waters. It has a speckled, lumpy body that enables it to lurk unseen amongst the stones on the seabed, waiting to grab passing prey.

Insect hide-and-seek

Insects have many enemies, so they are amongst the most effectively camouflaged creatures in the animal kingdom. They use a variety of different tricks to hide from attackers.

- One species of leaf insect has a flattened body and wings which look exactly like the leaves it feeds on. The disguise is so successful that the leaf insects sometimes try to eat each other!

- The Italian cricket can throw its voice, just like a ventriloquist, so its enemies never know where it is.

- Peppered moths living in polluted cities have turned dark brown. Members of the same species living in the countryside have stayed a speckled white colour.

35

Strange Animals

Male tree frog

Some animals have unique **abilities** or **body parts** that no other species possess. These individual features have usually been developed as ways of helping an animal to survive in one way or another. For instance, many creatures have unsual **defence mechanisms** to surprise their enemies.

Some creatures have unique body parts that help them to **feed** or to **survive** in harsh conditions.

Some animals are so extraordinary that scientists are still baffled by the reasons for their behaviour.

Amazing animals

Here are some animals with **unusual skills**:

- The tarsier can turn its head right round to look behind it without moving its body.

Tarsier

- When the three-banded armadillo is threatened by enemies, it rolls itself into a very tight armoured ball.

Curled-up armadillo

- A gorilla called Koko was taught by humans to use sign language. She used this skill to signal that she wanted a cat as a pet.

Koko the gorilla

- The Texas horned lizard can squirt blood out of its eyes, possibly as a form of defence against enemies.

Strange but true

- Guillemots can 'fly' underwater.

- Flies take off backwards.

- It takes an elephant calf six months to learn how to use its trunk.

- Crocodiles sometimes climb up trees.

Texas horned lizard

Hatchet fish

Stonefish

Arrow crab

● Most lizards have a tail that can break off if the lizard needs to escape from the grip of a predator. The tail is usually capable of growing again, at least once.

● Giraffes have 45-centimetre long black tongues which they can use to clean their ears.

Curious connections

Here are some strange animal **similarities**:

● The African elephant's closest relative is the hyrax, which is the size of a rabbit.

● The giraffe has seven neckbones, exactly the same number as a human.

Hyrax

Bizarre birds

Here are some unusual patterns of **bird** behaviour:

● Once the female Emperor penguin has laid an egg, the male keeps it warm by balancing it on his feet under a flap of skin.

● Some birds, such as the reed warbler, can sing two tunes at once.

Reed warbler

Hummingbird

● The hummingbird is the only bird that can fly backwards.

Fascinating fish

The **underwater world** is full of strange surprises:

● The arawana lives in the flooded Amazon rainforest. It can jump up to 2 metres out of the water to feed on small birds or bats in the trees above.

● The African lungfish lives in mud at the bottom of dried-out swamps. It burrows into the ground and covers itself with mucus to keep moist.

● Dolphins, whales and porpoises talk to each other with clicking and whistling noises.

37

Endangered Animals

Cuban crocodile

About 5000 animal species are **endangered**. This means that their numbers are decreasing and that they may die out forever.

An animal species that has disappeared is called **extinct**. The population of some animal species has become so low that they are almost certain to become extinct within the next 20 years.

The endangered panda.

Some animals' lives are threatened because their homes and food are being destroyed by **pollution**, **farming** or **building**. Some are **hunted** for their fur and meat. Sadly, there is a huge illegal trade in 'luxury' **animal products** such as rare animal skins and furs.

Land mammals

Although there are organizations to protect endangered wildlife, many animals are still being **poached**, which means that they are killed illegally. Here are some examples:

● The rhinoceros is poached for its horn, which some people believe makes good medicine. Since 1960 the world rhino population has dropped by 85 per cent.

● For many years the African elephant was hunted for its ivory tusks, used for jewellery and ornaments. Now the world ivory trade is banned.

Ivory goods

● In Africa, some restaurants serve gorilla steaks. Gorillas are also hunted because they can damage crops. The most endangered species is the mountain gorilla.

● The musk deer is poached for its musk gland, which is used to make perfumes and is said to help treat snake bites.

Marine threat

Harmful chemicals and **oil** find their way into the oceans, making them hazardous for ocean life. Some creatures may escape the pollution, only to become victims of other life-threatening dangers:

● Some countries hunt whales for scientific reasons, but sometimes the carcasses are used illegally for food, despite strict hunting laws.

● Many dolphins and other sea creatures die when they are trapped in huge fishing nets.

Dolphin

Blue whale

Sea otter
(Pacific coast)

Snow leopard
(Asia)

Lemur
(Madagascar)

Whooping crane
(North America)

Birds in danger

About one fifth of all the world's endangered species are **birds**. **Oil pollution** causes a large number of bird deaths, but many are **trapped** or **shot** by humans. Protection laws are hard to enforce.

Rare hyacinthine macaws

- Exotic birds are often captured illegally and sold worldwide as caged pets. Amongst the rarest species is the large hyacinthine macaw of the Brazilian rainforest.

A cormorant clogged with oil

- An estimated 300,000 seabirds died when oil was spilt from a tanker off Alaska in 1989.

- Several well-known species of fish may eventually disappear because of overfishing. If shoals are caught more quickly than the fish can reproduce, the numbers decline.

- Many turtles have been forced away from the beaches where they breed, as hotels and tourism take over. Sometimes turtles have been deliberately killed.

Loggerhead turtle

Herring shoal

Strange but true

- In Japan you can buy a pair of real turtleshell glasses for about £1000.

- Rare African gorillas are sometimes shot so that their hands can be used to make ashtrays.

- When a mother river dugong is killed, the tears of her young are bottled and sold as good luck potion.

Saving Animals

All over the world, groups of people are working to **protect** endangered animals and to limit fur, skin and ivory hunting.

Areas of land called **reserves** have been set aside to provide safe homes for rare animals. There are also underwater nature reserves, where scuba diving and fishing are limited.

Sometimes rare species are kept in **zoos**, where they can safely breed new generations. Occasionally some of these animals are released back into the wild to build up the species once more.

Strange but true

● The rare kakapo parrot lays one egg every four years.

● The coelacanth fish was thought to be extinct for 70 million years, until one was found alive in 1938.

● Insecticide pollution has been traced in the bodies of Antarctic penguins, thousands of kilometres from civilization.

Project tiger

Until recently, the **tiger** was one of the most threatened animal species in the world. In 1972 the Indian government and the Worldwide Fund for Nature launched **Operation Tiger**:

● Tiger reserves were set up across India and Asia to provide safe areas where hunting is banned. Here the animals can breed without disturbance.

● Thanks to the Operation Tiger project, the number of tigers in India alone has more than doubled to over 4000 since the opening of the reserve areas. The tiger is no longer top of the endangered species list, and numbers are continuing to grow.

Tiger reserves in India

● Thousands of people pay to visit the reserves every year. The money helps to maintain the land on the reserves and goes towards funding important research.

Bengal tiger

● The natural habitat of the panda is gradually being destroyed in south-western China. Wildlife groups are working to create reserves for them along the lines of the Operation Tiger project in India.

Zoo work

- The Arabian oryx became extinct in the wild 20 years ago. Surviving oryx were reared in Arizona, USA, and the species is now back in the wild.

Arabian oryx

- Several endangered monkey species have been bred in zoos. However, it is not always safe to release them back into the wild because their jungle homes are still being destroyed.

- The rare Chatham Island black robin was saved from extinction by New Zealand wildlife experts, who used tom tits to foster the robin chicks.

Chatham Island robin

Extinct animals

An animal is officially **extinct** if it has not been seen for over 50 years. Here are some animals forced into extinction by humans.

- The dodo bird once lived on Mauritius. It was killed off in the seventeenth century when humans arrived on the island.

Dodo bird

- The great auk was hunted to extinction in the North Atlantic. It disappeared in the 1500s.

Great auk

- The South African quagga looked like a zebra. It was hunted for food until it died out.

What you can do

Here are some things **you** can do to help protect wildlife:

- Do not buy endangered animal skins or ivory products.

- Never steal birds' eggs from nests.

- Join your local conservation group, to help conserve the wildlife that lives near you.

World Wide Fund For Nature badge

Wild Animals Facts and Lists

Wild cats

Wild cats are found in almost every continent of the world. This table shows where some wild cats live.

	Africa	Asia	Europe	North America	South America
Cheetah	●				
Jaguar					●
Leopard	●	●			
Lion	●	●			
Lynx	●	●	●	●	
Ocelot					●
Puma				●	●
Tiger		●			

Endangered and extinct animals

● Scientists believe that up to a third of all known plant and animal species may be extinct by the year 2500.

● Dinosaurs became extinct about 65 million years ago.

● The passenger pigeon from America was killed for food and became extinct in 1899.

Here are some more endangered animals:

Arabian oryx	Sand lizards
Cranes	Spiny anteaters
Crocodiles	Tasmanian wolves
Giant tortoises	The platypus
Golden cats	Tigers
Indian lions	Tragopan pheasants
Lynx	Wallabies
Rhinoceroses	Whales

The last dodo died in 1681

Pets and wild animals

Some wild animals are now often kept as pets:

The common European tortoise
The Australasian cockatiel
The Australian budgerigar
African and Asian waxbills
African and Asian gerbils
South American cavies, or guinea pigs
Asian and North European hamsters
(All present-day golden hamsters in capitivity are descended from a litter found in Syria in 1930.)

Flightless birds

Here are some examples of birds that cannot fly, even though they have wings:

Emus	Wattlebirds
Cassowaries	Ostriches
Penguins	Kakapo parrots

Burrowing animals

These animals live in burrows:

Mongooses	Congo eels
Aardwolves	Moles
Hyenas	Rabbits
Burrowing clams	Wombats
Fiddler crabs	

The foods animals eat

Here are some examples of animals that eat meat only (carnivores):

Anacondas	Polar bears
Crocodiles	Praying mantis
Eagles	Tigers
Komodo dragons	Lions

Here are some animals that eat plants and meat (omnivores):

Baboons	Cockroaches
Badgers	Common snapper
Bush babies	Earwigs
Bustards	Harvestmen spiders

These animals eat carrion (the remains of dead animals):

Carrion Beetles	Hyenas
Golden Eagles	Vultures

Pests

● Pests are creatures that destroy crops or other plants.

● Aphids are insects that carry plant diseases and damage plants by eating them.

● Quelea birds may damage whole fields of grain, partly because of the huge numbers that feed together.

● Locusts are a large kind of grasshopper. Some types of locust are among the world's most destructive pests, flying in huge swarms and eating any plant they land on.

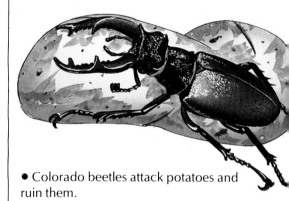

● Colorado beetles attack potatoes and ruin them.

Plant eaters

Here are some examples of animals that eat only plants:

Bears (except polar bears)
Green turtles
Iguanas
Emus
Gorillas
Rhinoceroses
Zebras
Antelopes
Elephants

Animal communication

Animals communicate with each other so that they can find food, or to attract a mate. This is how some animals communicate:

● Silk moths use their scent to attract a partner.

● Glow-worms have a green light that attracts other glow-worms.

- Mayflies swarm together and 'dance' over the water.

- Honey bees do an elaborate dance that directs the other bees to food.

- Ants leave trails to mark the route from their nest so they can return.

- Blue whales make sounds that can be heard by other whales up to 850 kilometres away.

- Squirrelfish make noises that can be heard even out of the water.

- Sticklebacks swim in a zig-zag pattern to attract females.

Changing shape

Here are some examples of animals that go through metamorphosis (change of shape) at different stages in their life:

Earwigs
Grasshoppers
Dragonflies
Butterflies
Moths
Flies

Migration

Some animals migrate (travel from one place to another) at certain times of the year to breed or find food. These are some examples:

- The North American monarch butterfly travels as far as Australia for the winter months.

- Salmon hatch in rivers and migrate to the sea, returning to their birthplace to breed.

- Eels migrate up to 5600 kilometres to reach their breeding grounds.

- Tuna fish travel long distances to reach the Mediterranean where they breed.

- Many birds migrate, but the Arctic tern travels furthest. It flies from the Arctic to the Antarctic, and back again, a trip of 32,000 kilometres.

Camouflage

Here are some examples of animals that can change colour quickly as a way of hiding from their enemies or prey:

Chameleons
Grouper fish
Flatfish
Octopuses
Tree frogs
Blossom spiders

Night-time animals

Nocturnal animals come out at night to feed or hunt, and rest during the day. These animals are nocturnal:

Many frogs and toads
Coral snakes
The Kakapo parrot
Owls
Nightjars
Opossums

Regrowing limbs

Here are some animals that can regrow parts of their bodies if damaged:

- Starfish can grow new 'arms'.

- Slow-worms can regrow broken-off tails.

- Lizards can grow new tails.

Whales

There are 90 species of whales, dolphins and porpoises. Here are some whales and their sizes:

Blue whale	30 metres
Grey whale	15 metres
Sperm whale	13 metres
Killer whale	6 metres
Pygmy sperm whale	4 metres
Narwhal	4 metres

Hibernation

- To hibernate means to go into a deep sleep through the winter.

- Newts, hedgehogs, bats and dormice hibernate over the winter.

- Only two kinds of birds hibernate, and they are both nightjars.

Desert creatures

This is how some desert animals survive:

- Camels store fat in their humps and water in their stomachs.

- The addax antelope does not need to drink very often.

- Jerboas burrow deep underground to keep away from the heat.

- Rhinoceroses bath in muddy water which then dries on them, protecting them from the Sun.

Biggest sea creatures

These are some of the largest creatures to be found in the sea, apart from whales:

Ribbon worm	54 metres
Whale shark	18 metres
Giant squid	17 metres
White shark	12 metres
Giant spider crab	3.65 metres
Starfish	1.37 metres
American lobster	1 metre

Dangerous animals

- One golden poison-dart frog could kill up to 1500 people with its poison.

- The mosquito carries diseases such as malaria, elephantiasis and yellow fever. Malaria kills over a million people a year.

- The great white shark is the most feared man-eating shark.

Wild Animals Facts and Lists

Reptiles

This table shows the average sizes of some reptiles:

Anaconda	9 metres
Reticulated python	9 metres
Saltwater crocodile	8 metres
King cobra	5.48 metres
Boa constrictor	4.26 metres
Mamba	2.13 metres
Leatherback turtle	2 metres
Grass snake	1 metre
Thread snake	114 mm
Gecko lizard	17 mm

This is how long it takes some reptile eggs to hatch:

Grass lizard	42 days
Marine turtle	55 days
Alligator	61 days
Python	61 days
Tortoise	105 days

Amazing eyes

● The giant squid has the largest eyes of any animal. They can be 39 cm across, which is 16 times wider than a human eye.

● A peregrine falcon can spot its prey from more than 8 km away.

● The golden eagle can spot its prey from over 3 km away.

Giant invertebrates

● The bird-eating spider from South America has a body as big as a child's hand.

● The African giant snail measures over 390 mm when fully grown.

● The Borneo dragonfly has a wingspan of 190 mm.

Birds

● There are about 100 billion birds in the world.

● There are 9000 species of birds.

● The North African ostrich is the tallest bird, at 2.74 metres.

Fast fliers

Spine-tailed swift	170 km/h
Pigeon	96 km/h
Hawk moth	53 km/h
Monarch butterfly	32 km/h
Honeybee	17 km/h

Beaks

The shape of birds' beaks gives a clue to the food they eat and how they eat it:

Hooked bills	eating flesh
Baggy beaks	scooping fish
Spear beaks	spearing fish
	spearing worms
Parrotbills	cracking seeds
Pointed beaks	spearing insects
	eating seeds
Crossbills	removing seeds from fir cone scales
Chisel beaks	boring nest holes and feeding
Tiny beaks	catching insects in the open mouth while flying

Wing shapes

Hovering birds	small, broad wings
Gliding birds	long, thin wings
Diving birds	wings fold back
Circling birds	long, wide wings
Dodging, diving birds	short, wide wings

Animal nests

Nests are made by many animals in lots of different ways:

● Swans make floating nests of reeds and sticks.

● Sticklebacks make nests using sand and weed.

● Swallows make nests using grasses woven or stuck together with mud and spit.

● Queen bumblebees often use old underground voles' nests in which they make a wax egg chamber.

● Siamese fighting fish make nests out of bubbles, which they hold together like shampoo froth.

● Eagles make the biggest nests. A bald eagle nest found in Florida, USA, in 1968 was 2.9 metres wide and 6 metres deep.

Treetop colonies

These birds make treetop nests in groups:

Crows
Herons
Storks
Pelicans
Weaver birds

Eggs

Here are the biggest and smallest bird egg sizes:

Ostrich	177 mm
Helena's hummingbird	12.7 mm

● After an egg has been laid, the time it takes to hatch is called its 'incubation time'.

Egg incubation times:

Finch	12 days
Thrush	14 days
Wren	16 days
Falcon	28 days
Ostrich	42 days
Hawk	44 days
Emperor penguin	63 days
Royal albatross	79 days

Animal sizes

These are the heights of some animals:

Giraffe	5.79 metres
African elephant	3.02 metres
Ostrich	2.74 metres
Brown bear	2.43 metres

Weights

Animal weights, from smallest to largest:

Bee hummingbird	1.4 grams
Mouse	22.4 grams
Goliath beetle	85 grams
Rat	455 grams
Marmoset	0.68 kg
Ringtail monkey	2.72 kg
Otter	5.89 kg
Armadillo	6.12 kg
Ocelot	19.27 kg
Porpoise	46.72 kg
Cheetah	57.83 kg
Alligator	57.83 kg
Llama	170 kg
Polar bear	324 kg
Moose	362 kg
Pilot whale	680 kg
Walrus	1625 kg
African elephant	7112 kg
Sperm whale	37,593 kg
Blue whale	155,963 kg

Animal pregnancies

This is how long some babies take to grow inside their mothers before they are born:

Opossum	13 days
House mouse	19 days
Chimpanzee	237 days
Camel	406 days
Giraffe	410 days
Rhinoceros	560 days
Indian elephant	624 days

Animal speeds

• The slowest land mammal is the three-toed sloth of tropical South America. Its average speed is 2.13 metres a minute.

• The sleepiest mammals are armadillos, sloths and opposums. They spend 80 per cent of their lives sleeping or dozing.

Animal lifespans

This is how long some animals live:

Mayfly	1 day
Mouse	2-3 yrs
Rattlesnake	18 yrs
Lion	25 yrs
Hippopotamus	40 yrs
Ostrich	50 yrs
African elephant	60 yrs
Dolphin	65 yrs
Rhinoceros	70 yrs
Tortoise	100 yrs

Animal skins

• Snakes and lizards have scaly skins. The rough scales underneath help a snake to move along. The skin is watertight, enabling snakes and lizards to live in or out of the water.

• Tortoises have developed their scaly skin into an armoured shell.

• Furry or feathered skins keep some animals warm in winter.

• Birds lose some of their feathers in the summer to keep cool.

• Birds such as penguins oil their feathers from an oil gland in their skin to waterproof themselves.

Animal feet

• Swans and ducks have webbed feet which they use as paddles when swimming.

• The blue-footed booby uses its webbed feet to incubate its eggs during breeding.

• Lizards, newts, gorillas and lemurs are examples of animals that have five toes on each foot. Toes are used for climbing and gripping.

• The elephant's foot is also five-toed, but is round and massive to support its weight.

History of how life began

The development of animals and plants has taken millions of years. The facts below shows this evolution as if it had happened in a year.

• January 1: the Earth forms.

• March 29: bacteria and other simple life forms appear.

• November 27: the first fish develop in the sea.

• December 15: the first dinosaurs appear.

• December 28: various mammals develop.

• December 31: the first ape-men appear. Modern humans develop just hours before the end of the year.

45

INDEX